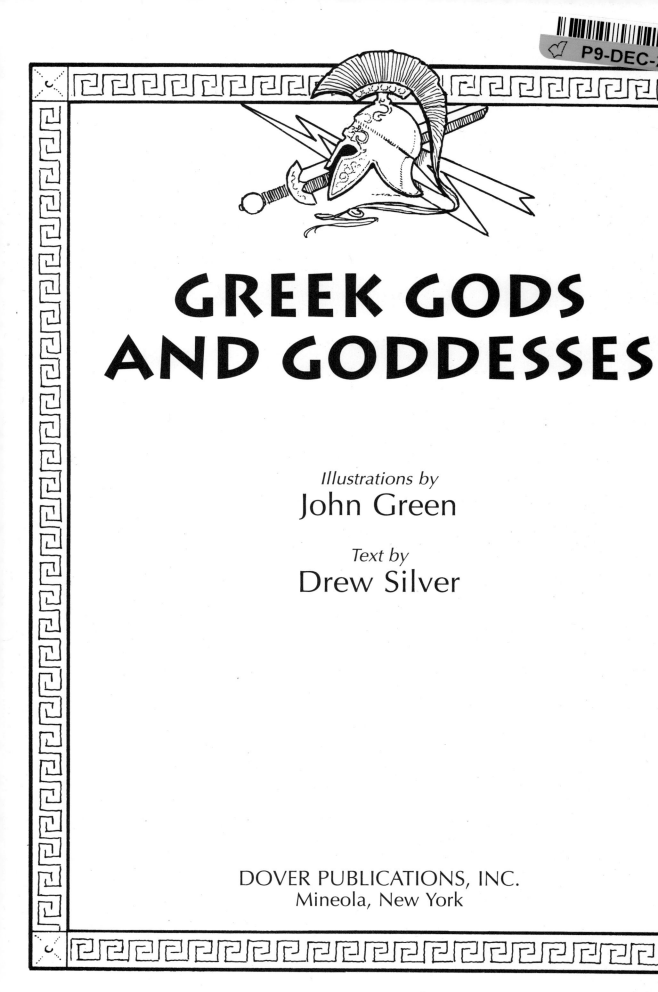

GREEK GODS AND GODDESSES

Illustrations by
John Green

Text by
Drew Silver

DOVER PUBLICATIONS, INC.
Mineola, New York

Bibliographical Note

Greek Gods and Goddesses is a new work, first published by Dover Publications, Inc., in 2001.

International Standard Book Number
ISBN-13: 978-0-486-41862-9
ISBN-10: 0-486-41862-6

Manufactured in the United States by Courier Corporation
41862606
www.doverpublications.com

NOTE

Ancient Greek mythology was part of a culture that lived for over a thousand years, with a prehistory reaching back millenia. It is an integral part of that culture's imaginative understanding of nature, human psychology, and its own history. It developed historically as a result of migrations, trade and absorption of local cults, and traditions; its figures, themes, and narratives show signs of origin in India, Asia Minor, Central Asia, the Middle East, and Egypt as well as in Greek territories. Greek mythology was absorbed and further modified by other cultures with which it came into contact, particularly that of Rome. In Greece, it was altered by oral transmission, adaptation by local cults, political manipulation, and of course imaginative folk and literary storytelling. (There never was a coherent religious structure in Greece, or a canon of religious writing.) All these processes resulted in variations and new stories that were incorporated into the body of myth and legend that has been transmitted to us.

Most of what we know of Greek religion, myth, and legend comes from such literary sources as Homer, Hesiod, the Homeric Hymns, Pindar and other poets, the dramatists, and such writers as Pausanias and Apollodorus, who compiled a *Library* of mythology around 150 BCE; from modern-day interpretation of vase paintings, architectural sculpture, and archaeological evidence; and from linguistic research, including the twentieth-century reading of previously undecipherable Middle Eastern inscriptions. The Romans, who for their own reasons adopted much of Greek religion and mythology, somewhat arbitrarily identifying many Latin and Italian deities and spirits with those of the Greeks and subtly or not so subtly modifying them, have also influenced our understanding of the Greek material, either directly through Roman poets such as Ovid, or by way of Byzantine, medieval Church, or Renaissance writers.

In this little book we can do no more than hint at the great literary and historical interest of Greek mythology. Here we present basic versions of narratives that were known to the Greeks in the Classical period, roughly between 700 and 350 BCE, with variations noted. An exception is the story of Cupid and Psyche, which is the work of a Roman writer of the second century CE. We present it as an example of the creative life led by Greek myths outside the Greek world.

A note on dates: the terms "CE" (of the common era) and "BCE" (before the common era) are the now-standard terms corresponding to "AD" and "BC."

1. *Kronos attacks his father Ouranos with a scythe.*

The Greek creation myth, as related by Hesiod, says that out of Chaos (the void) came the originary deities Gaia (Earth), Erebos (darkness), Nyx (night) and Eros (love). Gaia then bore Ouranos (heaven or sky). Ouranos became the supreme ruler of the universe and, under the influence of Eros, mated with Gaia to become the father of the Titans, the Hekatoncheires (the hundred-armed giants), and the Kyklopes.

Ouranos, according to the story, hated and feared all his children, and imprisoned them in Tartaros, a chamber deep in the Earth—that is, in the body of Gaia—to protect himself from them.

Gaia, distressed and angry, urged her imprisoned children to act against the tyrannical Ouranos. Only the Titan Kronos agreed. Gaia supplied him with a scythe, or sickle, and concealed him near her bed; when Ouranos came to her, Kronos attacked him. He castrated Ouranos and threw the severed parts into the sea; from the drops of blood that fell on Gaia, the Gigantes (Giants), the Erinyes (Furies) and the Melian nymphs were born; from the foam raised by the severed members falling into the sea was born the goddess Aphrodite (*aphros*: "foam").

Kronos replaced his father as supreme ruler and freed his brother and sister Titans from Tartaros—but reimprisoned the Kyklopes and the Hekatoncheires.

The sketchiness of this story may reflect its importation from Asian sources, in which Ouranos and Gaia were more integral figures to the local religious cults. Neither they nor Kronos were important figures in Greek mythology and were never subjects of religious cults in Greece.

KRONOS
Kronos attacking Ouranos.

2. ***Rheia*** *gives the baby Zeus to the Melian nymphs to hide from Kronos.*

After Kronos violently supplanted his father Ouranos, he freed his brother and sister Titans, and took his sister Rheia as his wife.

The enraged Ouranos cursed Kronos, and prophesied that the same thing would happen to him—that Kronos would be overthrown by one of his own children. To keep this from happening, Kronos devoured each of his children as soon as they were born. Hestia, Demeter, Hera, Hades, Poseidon—shortly after the birth of each, Kronos came to Rheia and demanded that she hand the child over, and one after the other, he swallowed all five. When Rheia was about to give birth for the sixth time, however, she went to Crete and hid in a cave until the child was born. The baby's cries were concealed by her attendants, the Kuretes, who performed noisy ritual dances. When Rheia returned to Olympos she deceived Kronos by giving him instead of the child a stone wrapped in swaddling clothes, which he swallowed without examining. Zeus she entrusted to the Melian nymphs, who brought him up on Mt. Ida. (In Homer, Zeus is the oldest, not the youngest, of the children of Kronos and Rheia.)

Eventually, Zeus fulfilled the prophecy of Ouranos and overthrew his father Kronos. Zeus became the most powerful god, the ruler over all others; his symbol, the thunderbolt. He was concerned with order, justice, and honesty; in Homer, he was "cloud-gathering Zeus," "father of gods and men."

RHEIA

Rheia giving the baby Zeus to the nymphs Adrasta and Ida.

3. *Zeus* hurls thunderbolts at the Titans during the war for supremacy.

So that Zeus might live, Kronos had been tricked into swallowing a stone instead of the baby Zeus. He eventually became aware of Zeus's continued existence, but as Ouranos had predicted, was unable to prevent Zeus's attacking and defeating him.

Zeus compelled Kronos to swallow a potion that forced him to disgorge the children he had swallowed, as well as the stone that Rheia had substituted for Zeus.

Kronos and the Titans did not all submit to Zeus and fought bitterly for supremacy against the Olympian gods. Neither side was able to gain an advantage in this war, which raged on the plains of Thessaly. Finally, at Rheia's urging, Zeus turned for help to the siblings of Kronos whom Kronos had not freed, the Kyklopes and the hundred-armed Hekatoncheires. The Kyklopes knew how to make thunderbolts, against which there was no defense; Zeus hurled these and caused panic among the Titans, and the Hekatoncheires, each able to throw a hundred rocks at a time, pursued them down into Tartaros. There Zeus imprisoned them, with the Hekatoncheires as their jailers. This was the end of the war, known as the Titanomachy, which had lasted for ten years.

Zeus then became, like his father, the chief of the gods, but unlike the tyrannical Kronos, he shared responsibilities with his siblings. In one version of this story Zeus and his brothers cast lots to determine where each would rule; Zeus's portion was the heavens, Poseidon's the sea, Hades's the Underworld. Like Kronos, Zeus took a sister, Hera, for his consort. He produced many children, both gods and mortals. His divine offspring included Ares, Athena, Apollo, Artemis, Hebe, Hermes, and Dionysos. Aphrodite, another offspring of Ouranos, was also an Olympian. The stone that Kronos had swallowed and been forced to disgorge was placed at Delphi to mark the center of the world.

ZEUS
Zeus hurling thunderbolts at the Titans.

4. **Atlas,** *forced to hold up the heavens as punishment for his part in the Titanomachy.*

Atlas was a Titan, son of Iapetos, grandson of Ouranos, nephew of Kronos and the brother of Prometheos and Epimetheos. He was the guardian of the pillars that held up the sky. Atlas took part in the Titanomachy, the ten-year war waged by the Titans against Zeus and the Olympian gods after Zeus overthrew Kronos. After the victory of the gods, most of the Titans were relegated to Tartaros, the deepest pit in the earth, as far below the Underworld, it was said, as the sky is above the earth. Atlas's punishment was different—he was compelled by Zeus to hold up the sky by himself.

Atlas came to be identified with the mountains of western North Africa, now known as the Atlas Mountains.

One of the labors imposed on the half-mortal hero Herakles was to find and bring to his master Eurystheos the Golden Apples of Hesperides, which were grown in a garden on an island past the end of the world (in the Atlantic, west of what are now known as the Gates of Hercules). One version of this story says that Herakles induced Atlas to find the apples for him while he took Atlas's place supporting the heavens. When Atlas returned, he refused to take up his burden again, and Herakles had to trick him into doing so.

ATLAS
Atlas shouldering his eternal burden.

5. **_Hephaistos_** _at his forge inside Mt. Etna, as Athena looks on._

Hephaistos was the god of fire and of crafts and the son of Hera. In Hesiod, the jealous Hera conceived and bore him alone, in response to the birth of Athena from the head of Zeus. It is thought that Hephaistos may have been an eastern deity introduced into Greece along with the knowledge of metalworking. His forge was said to be in Mt. Etna, in Sicily. In Homer, he is the maker of the shield of Achilles; in Hesiod, he is the creator of the first woman, Pandora, through whom all ills and sorrows came to humanity.

Hephaistos was ugly and lame. In one version of his story, he took his mother's side in a dispute (over her persecution of Zeus's son Herakles) between her and Zeus; Zeus took him by the foot and threw him to earth, where after falling for an entire day he crashed on the island of Lemnos. In another version, Hephaistos is deformed at birth, and Hera herself threw him into the sea. He later took revenge when he built a throne for her that held her captive when she sat in it. He would not free her until Dionysos made him drunk and forced him to do so.

Hephaistos was given permission by Zeus to marry his daughter Athena, goddess of wisdom, but Athena, who is always represented as a virgin, rejected him. He attempted unsuccessfully to take her by force; as he did so he spilled his seed on the earth, engendering Erechthonios, who had the body of a serpent. Athena gave him to the daughters of the mythical first king of Athens, Kekrops, to raise, and in time he too became king.

HEPHAISTOS
Hephaistos with a resentful Athena.

6. **Hera** *confronts Zeus over the maiden Io, transformed into a cow.*

Hera, sister and wife of Zeus and queen of the Olympian gods, was important in Greek religion, and her cult was widespread. Although the mother of Ares, Hephaistos, and Hebe (goddess of youth), and goddess of marriage and childbirth, she was a virgin; she recovered her virginity every year by bathing in a magical spring. Her primary attributes were jealousy and vindictiveness; she was jealous and angry at Zeus's constant infidelities and suspicious and undeceived by his attempts to mislead her. She devoted much energy to persecuting his lovers and their children by him. In the *Iliad,* she supported the Greek side against Troy in the Trojan War.

Io was a priestess of Hera, a mortal although the daughter of a river god, Inachos, the mythical first king of Argos. She was pursued by Zeus, who came to her in dreams. Her troubled father consulted oracles and was told that he must banish her from Argos. When he did, Hera turned Io into a cow—at which Zeus transformed himself into a bull. Hera then sent a Fury in the form of a gadfly to sting Io continuously to keep her moving.

The best-known version of Io's story is not Greek but comes from Ovid, the Roman poet. In this version, Zeus—one of whose Homeric epithets is "cloud-gatherer"—spreads a dark cloud over the place where he has a tryst with Io, to prevent Hera from seeing. Hera is suspicious, however, and goes to investigate. Just before she arrives, Zeus turns Io into a cow, but Hera, who is not deceived, asks him for it as a gift. Zeus cannot say no. Hera then sets her herdsman, the many-eyed Argos, to watch over it.

HERA

Hera confronting Zeus over Io, whom Zeus has transformed into a cow.

7.   **Hermes** *slays the many-eyed Argos as he sleeps.*

Hermes was the son of Zeus and Maia, eldest of the Pleiades, the daughters of Atlas. He was the messenger of Zeus and herald of the gods; he was the god of travelers, roads and boundaries, of luck, of sleep and of dreams; he was a trickster, clever, furtive, and devious. As the god of boundaries, he ruled communications, and therefore speech and oratory. He guided the souls of the newly dead to the Underworld; he was also the patron of merchants, thieves, and athletes. His name derives from *herma,* a pile of stones used as a boundary marker. His monuments, called *herms,* were also built by roadsides and often included a sculpted phallus. He is usually shown with winged shoes and a winged broad-brimmed hat, and he carried a staff with miraculous properties—a kind of magic wand—known as a *kerykeion,* which has two snakes entwined around it. As Zeus's messenger he was fast-moving; in Homer he is called "speedy-comer."

When Zeus turned over Io, who had been transformed into a cow, to the jealous and suspicious Hera, she set the herdsman Argos (called Panoptes, "all-seeing") to guard her. Argos was a giant with a hundred eyes, some of which were always open; in some depictions, he had faces on both sides of his head. Zeus, knowing cleverness would be necessary, sent Hermes to free Io. Hermes disguised himself as a herdsman and lulled Argos to sleep, closing all his eyes, by playing music for him; in one version of the story, he then smashed Argos's head with a stone; in another, beheaded him with a sword. Hera put Argo's eyes in the tail of her peacock. She also sent a Fury, in the form of a gadfly, to sting Io continuously so that she would not be able to rest and would stay out of the hands of Zeus.

HERMES

Hermes slaying the many-eyed Argos.

8. **Ares,** *in full battle array, fights the Giants Otos and Ephialtes.*

Ares was the Greek god of war, son of Zeus and Hera. Unlike the Roman god Mars, with whom he was identified by the Romans, he was not an important, admired—Hesiod speaks of his "lamentable works"—or even very dignified figure. He represented not the martial virtues so admired by the Romans but the spirit of brutality, of violence and belligerence. He takes pleasure in battle, but is incapable of strategy and is vulnerable to those shrewder or more intelligent than he, including mortals. He was the father of several children by Aphrodite.

Otos and Ephialtes, also known as the Aloidai (they were sons of Aloidos) were two giants, said to have been eighteen yards tall by the time they were nine. They are characterized as insanely insolent, committing criminal effronteries and outrages against the gods out of grandiose ambition. In Homer they are said to have captured Ares and imprisoned him in a bronze jar for thirteen months until he was freed by Hermes. They piled Ossa upon Pelion—that is, a mountain upon another mountain—in an attempt to reach the heavens so that they might attack and overthrow the gods. Zeus destroyed them.

The giants Otos and Ephialtes were sometimes confused with the Giants, a race of monsters born of the drops of blood that spilled on Gaia, the earth, when Kronos castrated his father Ouranos. As a result Otos and Ephialtes sometimes appear in depictions of the Battle of Gods and Giants, or Gigantomachy, a late myth in which the Giants rebelled against the gods, were defeated, and were buried beneath volcanoes.

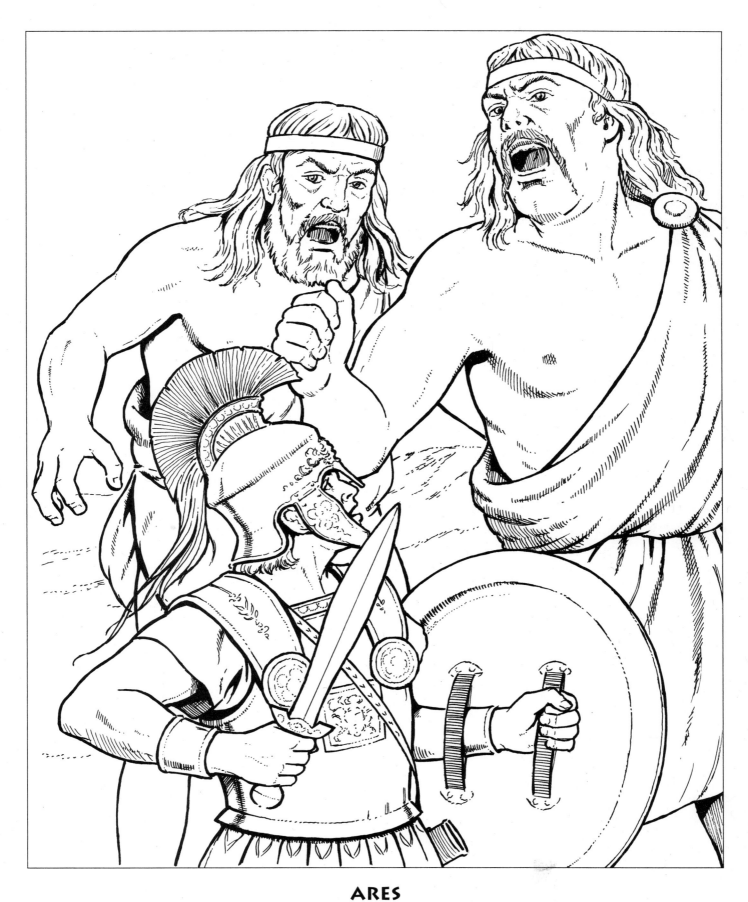

ARES

A scene from the Gigantomachy, in which the god Ares fights Otos and Ephialtes, who in this version are not merely giants but Giants.

9. **Prometheos,** *chained to a rock and eternally torn by an eagle.*

Prometheos was a son of the Titan Iapetos, and the brother of Atlas and Epimetheos. According to Hesiod he was the creator of the human race (as Epimetheos was the creator of the animals).

In the Titanomachy, the war for supremacy waged by the Titans against the Olympian gods, Prometheos attempted to advise his fellow Titans (his name means "forethought"; that of his brother Epimetheos means "afterthought") but was disregarded, and he changed sides. Even so, his independent character made him unable to subordinate himself to Zeus.

In Hesiod, Prometheos had created men out of clay, and Athena had given them life. Zeus, who feared that men would become too powerful, ordered that fire be forbidden them, but Prometheos gave them not only fire (stolen, depending on the version, either from heaven or from Hephaistos's forge) but various kinds of useful knowledge with which to ease their lives. Zeus was enraged by this disobedience, and had Prometheos seized and bound to a rock high on a mountain, usually supposed to be in the Caucasus. Each day he sent an eagle to tear out and devour Prometheos's liver. Each night it grew back. Prometheos was eventually freed by Herakles.

In the version given by Aischylos, Prometheos, from his rock, taunts Zeus and refuses to tell him the secret of his survival (Prometheos is a Titan and therefore immortal); in retaliation, Zeus hurls a thunderbolt at him, blasting him to Tartaros, where he is trapped for thirty thousand years. (Unfortunately the means by which he escapes from this predicament was revealed in a work that is now lost.)

While Prometheos was thus being punished, Zeus found another way to ensure that mankind did not become too godlike: he had Hephaistos fashion the first woman, Pandora, through whom all the ills of humanity were released into the world.

PROMETHEOS
Prometheos on his rock, watched by the eagle of Zeus.

10. *Athena* wins possession of Attica in a contest with *Poseidon.*

Athena was the daughter of Zeus and the goddess of wisdom, of war, of cities, and of crafts such as spinning and weaving. A beautiful virgin goddess, she was an enthusiastic warrior, usually represented with a spear and shield and wearing armor, including the *aegis,* a breastplate with a Gorgon's head and a fringe of snakes, and often with an owl on her shoulder. She was loyal to those who were just and courageous. Believed to be originally a prehellenic deity, Athena was one of the most important goddesses, the object of a widespread cult in Greece.

Athena was the daughter of Zeus and Metis ("counsel"), said by Hesiod to be Zeus's first wife. Fearing that his children by her would be a danger to him by virtue of their intelligence, he swallowed Metis. When it was time for Athena to be born, Hephaistos broke open Zeus's head with an ax and Athena emerged, fully grown and fully armed. (Metis did not reemerge, but by swallowing her Zeus is said to have acquired her wisdom.) She was said to be Zeus's favorite child.

Poseidon, god of the sea, brother of Zeus and almost as powerful, challenged Athena for ownership of Athens and of Attica. A contest was held between them on the Acropolis, judged by the first king of Athens, Kekrops, a man with the lower body of a serpent or fish. The winner was to be the one who produced the most useful gift for the people. Poseidon struck a rock and produced a saltwater spring; Athena won by bringing forth the olive tree. She became the patron goddess of Athens.

In the classical era, the Acropolis became the site of the Parthenon, the great temple to Athena.

ATHENA
Athena presenting the olive tree to the people of Attica.

11. **Aphrodite** kneels over the body of Adonis, killed by a wild boar.

Aphrodite was the goddess of love and beauty. According to Hesiod she was born from the foam (*aphros:* "foam") that formed around the severed genitals of Ouranos that had been flung into the sea by Kronos; she arose fully grown from the sea near Cyprus. (It is thought that she was originally an eastern deity and that her cult entered Greece through Cyprus.) According to Homer she was the daughter of Zeus and Dione, a goddess whose name is the feminine form of "Zeus." In Homer she was the wife of Hephaistos, god of fire and crafts.

Aphrodite embodied erotic love rather than affection and tenderness, and was often regarded as irresponsible and selfish. She was not faithful to Hephaistos; she lay with Ares whenever Hephaistos was away, and bore him several children. When Hephaistos discovered them in bed together, he trapped them there with a specially-made device and displayed them for the amusement of the other gods on Olympos.

Adonis, another god of eastern origin (his name, like the Hebrew *Adonai,* is derived from a Semitic root meaning "the Lord"), appears only in connection with Aphrodite. He is said to have been born from the trunk of a myrrh tree (into which his mother had been transformed as a consequence of the incestuous relationship into which she had tricked her father, who became Adonis's father) and to have been raised by nymphs. Aphrodite fell in love with him because he was so beautiful. Persephone also loved him, and, in different variations of the story, either Zeus or the muse Kalliope decreed that he should spend part of the year with each.

During his time with Aphrodite, against her warning, Adonis went hunting in the forest and was killed by a charging wild boar. Aphrodite was so grief-stricken that she caused the red anemone to bloom from his blood.

APHRODITE
Aphrodite grieving over the body of Adonis.

12. *Hades abducts Persephone in his chariot.*

Hades was the god of the dead and ruler of the Underworld. He was a son of Kronos and Rheia, and brother of Zeus and Poseidon. He was grim, without compassion or mercy, but was not hostile, to men or gods. He was sometimes euphemistically called Plouton ("wealth-giver"), since both crops and metals come from underground.

Persephone, known to the Greeks more usually as Kore ("daughter" or "maiden"), was Zeus's daughter by his sister Demeter, goddess of agriculture and fertility.

Hades wished to marry Persephone, who was extremely beautiful. Demeter, who preferred to live on earth rather than on Olympos, did not approve. She was protective of Persephone and kept her far away from the other gods, by tradition in Enna in Sicily. One day when Persephone was in a meadow picking flowers, she plucked a dark blue narcissus that had been placed there by Zeus. An opening in the earth appeared and Hades burst forth in his chariot pulled by dark blue horses; he seized Persephone and took her to the Underworld. There she yearned only for her mother and would eat nothing. Demeter's horror and grief were so great that she neglected everything to search for Persephone, causing drought and famine all over the earth, and especially in Sicily.

The myths of Demeter and Persephone are connected with fertility and the seasons. The adbuction of Persephone is related to the period in which the earth becomes barren and seed must be buried in the soil before returning in the form of growing grain.

HADES
Hades abducting Persephone in his chariot.

13. *Hermes brings Persephone back from the Underworld to her mother **Demeter.***

Demeter ("Mother Earth") was a daughter of Kronos and Rheia and sister of Zeus and Hades. She was goddess of the harvest and of agriculture generally. She preferred to spend her time on earth rather than on Olympos.

Demeter was the mother of Persephone, who had been abducted by Hades and taken to the Underworld. Demeter's grief, and her sense of having been dishonored, were so great that she caused drought and famine to afflict the earth. Demeter searched all over the world, carrying a torch and ignoring all pleas from the gods to return to her duties. In one account, she was taken to Helios, god of the sun, who sees everything, and from him discovered Persephone's whereabouts.

Because the earth was becoming dry and barren, and sacrifice to the gods would soon become impossible, Zeus decided to help Demeter; he sent Hermes to bring Persephone back—on condition that she eat nothing while in the Underworld. Until then, she had not, but Hades, who agreed to release her, gave her a pomegranate for the return trip, and when she was brought to Zeus she admitted that she had eaten a few seeds. So Zeus commanded that she spend the summer months with Hades in the Underworld, and the rest on earth with Demeter. That is how Persephone became both Queen of the Dead and a fertility goddess.

The myth of Persephone embodies the cycle of barrenness and growth in nature. The Eleusinian Mysteries, of which Demeter is goddess, celebrated this cycle as well. Demeter was said to have founded the cult to commemorate her success in liberating Persephone from the earth; devotees believed that the story showed that from death, new life would come.

DEMETER

Hermes bringing Persephone from the Underworld to a waiting Demeter.

14. *Dionysos* surrounded by his followers, including maenads, nymphs and satyrs.

Dionysos (sometimes called Bacchus, an alternative name that originated in Asia Minor) was the god of wine and ecstatic abandon. He was the son of Zeus and Semele, the daughter of Cadmus, king of Thebes. The jealous Hera destroyed Semele by convincing her to ask Zeus to reveal himself to her in all his divine strength and power, knowing that the experience would be more than Semele, a mortal, could withstand. Semele was struck by a thunderbolt and burnt to ashes. Zeus put the unborn Dionysos in his thigh, from which he was later born.

Dionysos was a late addition to the Olympian pantheon, although it is believed that his cult predates those of the major Greek deities. Although he eventually became one of the most important deities of the Hellenic period, his cult earlier encountered suppression and resistance, as dangerous and subversive, from the elites who ruled the Greek states. Many stories told of him deal with resistance to his worship and his punishment of those of those who have rejected him.

Dionysos was credited with the first cultivation of grapevines and the invention of wine. He revealed himself through intoxication and ecstasy; he increased clarity, lessened anxiety, and inspired self-abandon and forgetfulness of mortality. To those who resisted him he brought destruction; among his followers he inspired frenzy. His worshipers engaged in ecstatic celebrations and orgies, roaming the countryside playing music, dancing and sometimes tearing apart wild animals and eating them raw, an act believed to bring about the incorporation of the god's spirit. This is unique among Greek religious cults.

Dionysos is usually represented accompanied by satyrs and maenads ("frenzied [or mad] women," sometimes called bacchantes), dressed in fawn skins and carrying torches, snakes and *thyrsoi* (staffs decorated with ivy and grape leaves and topped with pinecones).

DIONYSOS
Dionysos reclining with a cup of wine as his companions revel.

15. *Apollo slays the serpent Python.*

Apollo was the son of Zeus and Leto, a Titan, and the twin brother of Artemis. He was the great god of prophecy, and his greatest shrine was at Delphi, where he was the patron god of the most important Greek oracle. He was the god of healing, though also associated with plagues, and of the arts, especially music; he was the patron of archers and archery, though neither of war nor hunting; he was the protector of herds and herdsmen, though associated with the wolf. He is also associated with light and, in later times, with the sun.

For the Greeks, Apollo represented the benefits of civilization. He embodied the qualities that classical Greek culture most admired; he was beautiful, young, athletic, mature, rational, and cultivated. In some stories, however, he is represented as cruel and merciless.

According to the Apollo myth, Hera, the jealous wife of Zeus, sent Python—a monstrous serpent formed from the slime left by the great deluge—to prevent Leto from giving birth. Leto fled to the island of Delos, the only place willing to allow a birth opposed by Hera. Here Artemis and Apollo were born, after a labor of nine days. Delos was sacred to Apollo and one of his major shrines was located there.

Apollo was full-grown within days of his birth. Because of its persecution of his mother (or, alternatively, because it spread terror among mortals) he pursued Python to Delphi, where it guarded (or in some versions, was) the oracle, and killed it. He then took control of the oracle, but since Python had been the child of Gaia (Earth), he had to propitiate her, which he did by renaming the oracle Pythia and founding the Pythian Games in her honor. This story most likely reflects the history of the Apollo cult's replacement of an earlier Pythian cult.

APOLLO
Apollo having just slain the serpent Python.

16. *Artemis, with her nymphs, hunts a stag in the woods.*

Artemis was the daughter of Zeus and Leto and twin sister of Apollo. Goddess and protector of wildlife and fertility, she was also goddess of archery and hunting. She was said to be the protector of young women, of babies and of women in childbirth (as was Hera also). Though she apparently originated as an earth mother or fertility goddess (and was often confused or identified with other, similar deities), by classical times she was a virgin. Artemis strenuously guarded her virginity, and was attended by a retinue of nymphs whom she required also to be virgins. She was said to have killed the giant Orion, who challenged her; she was also said to have turned one of her nymphs, Kallisto, into a bear because Kallisto had had a child by Zeus, although in other versions Kallisto was transformed by the jealous Hera.

In the *Iliad,* Homer presents Artemis as supporting the Trojans, which brought her into conflict with Hera. Hera berated Artemis for interfering in matters of warfare, and struck her with her own quiver. Artemis fled weeping as her mother Leto gathered up the arrows.

ARTEMIS

Artemis hunting a stag.

17. *The Muses* gathered on Mt. Parnassos.

The Muses were the daughters of Zeus and Mnemosyne ("Memory") and were the goddesses of the arts of music, literature, and dance, and later of all intellectual endeavors such as history and philosophy. Originally there were three Muses, named Melete ("Practice"), Mneme ("Memory") and Aoide ("Song"). Hesiod names nine, but not until much later, in Roman times, were they associated with particular activities. The Muses were subordinate to Apollo, the god of prophecy and the arts. They are often depicted as winged.

The Muses were said variously to have lived in Pieria, on the slopes of Olympos, or on Mount Helikon. Hesiod himself lived beneath Mount Helikon and he begins his long poem the *Theogony,* the source of so much of our knowledge of Greek mythology, by explaining that he met the Muses on the mountainside and was inspired by them to write his account of the gods. Mount Parnassos was also sacred both to Apollo and to the Muses.

Ancient Greek poets, artists, and musicians credited the Muses as the source of their gifts and their inspiration. It was common for poets to invoke them, as Homer, like Hesiod, does at the start of both the Iliad ("Sing, O Goddess, the anger of Achilles . . . ") and the *Odyssey* ("Speak to me, Muse, of the adventurous man . . . ").

The nine Muses of Hesiod, and the arts with which they were later associated, are Kalliope (epic poetry), Klio (history), Erato (lyric poetry and song), Euterpe (flute playing), Melpomene (tragedy), Polymnia (hymns, and later, mime), Terpsichore (choral singing and dancing), Thalia (comedy), and Ourania (astronomy).

THE MUSES

The Muses—without wings—gathered on Helikon or Parnassos.

18. *Pan sits by a stream, playing the syrinx.*

Pan was the god of the pastoral and the rural, of pastures and flocks, of shepherds and goatherds, and of wild mountainsides and valleys. His father was usually said to be Hermes, but sometimes Zeus, Apollo, or another god; his mother usually a nymph. He had the legs and feet of a goat, and horns on his head—the medieval image of the devil is said to be derived from representations of Pan—and was ugly, noisy, dirty, crude, foul-smelling, earthy, and lustful. He lived in Arcadia, the center of his cult (and whose name, in Western culture, has come to stand for the rustic and bucolic), and was a favorite of the other gods.

Pan is also associated with terror. Some believed that Pan had caused the Persians to flee in panic (*panikos:* "of Pan") at the battle of Marathon, and a shrine was established to him as a result.

Pan spent much of his time in the countryside lustfully pursuing nymphs. He became especially infatuated with a naiad (water nymph) named Syrinx, an ardent devotee and imitator of Artemis. Like Artemis, she was a zealous defender of her virginity, and fled from Pan's unwanted attention. This only caused him to pursue her more strenuously across the woods and meadows. Finally she came to a river, which she was unable to cross; despairing, she prayed to the river nymphs for assistance. They instantly transformed her into a bed of reeds at the river's edge. Since the reeds were all he could have of her, Pan cut some of them in various lengths and bound them together, sealed with wax, to make a musical instrument which he played in her honor, or to accompany the nymphs in their dancing. This instrument is known as a syrinx or pan pipe.

PAN

Pan playing his syrinx by the side of a stream.

19. *Eos streaks across the sky in her chariot.*

Eos was the goddess of dawn. (In Hesiod, she is Erigenia, "early-born" or "early-comer"; in Homer she is "yellow-robed," "rosy-fingered.") She was the daughter of the Titans Hyperion and Theia, and the sister of Helios, the sun god, and Selene, the moon goddess. By her husband Astraios she was the mother of Zephyros, Boreas, and Notos (the winds), of Eosphoros ("dawn-bringer," the morning star), Hesperos (the evening star), and Astra (the stars).

Each day Eos rose from the island of Aiaia, in the river Okeanos that encircled the world, and rode across the sky in a golden chariot pulled by winged horses, accompanied by her brother Helios.

Eos slept with Ares, for which she was cursed by Aphrodite, who caused her to conceive a passion for one young mortal man after another. One of these was Orion, who was killed by Artemis. Another was Kephalos, by whom she bore Phaiton. Yet another was Tithonos, whom she married; he was the son of Laomedon, king of Troy, and the brother of Priam. Eos asked Zeus to grant him immortality, and he did; but she failed to ask for eternal youth, and Tithonos continued to age until he was as shriveled and dried up as a cicada, and eventually Eos abandoned him. Tithonos and Eos fathered two sons, Memnon, king of Ethiopia, who was killed in the Trojan War, and Emathion.

EOS

Eos crossing the sky in her chariot.

20. *Aiolos* giving Odysseos a bag containing the unruly winds.

Aiolos was a mortal, king of Aiolia. In some versions of his story, he had been a sailor who had invented sails and was able to predict the weather. In Homer, Aiolos was dear to the gods, and Zeus had made him steward of the winds, with the power to control them at will. In a later period he was sometimes thought of as the god of the winds.

In the *Odyssey*, Odysseos and his men, after making their escape from the Kyklops Polyphemos, arrived on Aiolia, a floating island surrounded by a wall of bronze. They were received with great, abundant hospitality by Aiolos, his queen, and his six sons and six daughters. After a month of continual feasting and telling of stories about the Trojan War, Odysseos asked Aiolos's help in returning home. Aiolos provisioned him generously, and gave him a special leather bag—Homer tells us that he flayed a nine-year-old ox to make it—in which he had bound the winds, and tied it to Odysseos's ship with a silver cord so they could not blow the ship off course. He then summoned the west wind to propel Odysseos home.

After nine days' sailing Odysseos and his men were within sight of Ithaka, so close that they could see men tending fires in the fields. But now the men had become resentful. They suspected that Aiolos's leather bag contained a treasure Odysseos was not sharing with them, though all had borne their journey's hardships equally; and when Odysseos slept, they opened it. Out rushed the winds, creating a storm that blew them all the way back to Aiolia. When Aiolios, who was astonished to see them, was told what had happened, he ordered them to leave his island at once. He understood that behind the misfortune of Odysseos and his men lay the gods, and he would not help anyone "detested by the blessed gods."

AIOLOS
Aiolos giving Odysseos the leather bag containing the unruly winds.

21. ***Poseidon*** *rises up out of the sea and creates a storm that shipwrecks Odysseos.*

Poseidon was the god of the sea. He was hostile, ill-tempered, violent, and destructive—called "earthshaker" in Homer, he was the god of sea-storms and earthquakes—and was the most powerful god after Zeus, who was his younger brother. Represented as tall, bearded, and fearsome, in Greek art he is frequently indistinguishable from Zeus. He is usually shown holding a trident, a three-pointed spear.

Among Poseidon's many children were the Kyklops Polyphemos, who in Homer's *Odyssey* was blinded by Odysseos. This act earned Odysseos Poseidon's undying hatred.

Journeying home from the Trojan War, Odysseos and his companions came to the island of Helios, the god of the sun. His tired and hungry men committed the sacrilege of killing and eating cattle from the sacred herds that were kept there. Helios demanded that Zeus take vengeance. As the men departed the island, Zeus destroyed their ship with a thunderbolt, killing them all but Odysseos, who alone had not taken part in the slaughter. Clinging to the wreckage, Odysseos floated to the island of Ogygia, home of the goddess Kalypso, who kept him for seven years and promised to make him immortal if he married her. Odysseos refused, and commanded by Zeus, after an appeal from Athena, Kalypso finally gave him men and material to build a vessel and allowed him to go. As Odysseos sailed away he was seen by Poseidon, now his enemy. Poseidon raised a huge storm that wrecked the craft. With the help of the goddess Leukotheia, Odysseos eventually washed up on the Phaiakan shore. The seafaring Phaiakans assisted him by giving him a ship that could go anywhere in a few hours, and on it Odysseos finally returned to Ithaka. On its return to Phaiaka Poseidon turned the ship to stone and sank it.

POSEIDON
Poseidon rising angrily and striking the sea with his trident,
causing a violent storm that overwhelms Odysseos's craft.

22. *Psyche* gazes for the first time on the face of her slumbering lover Cupid.

The story of Cupid and Psyche is not Greek, but shows Greek myth near the beginning of its long afterlife as a source of literary imagery in European culture.

In Hesiod, Eros emerged from Chaos (the Void) at the beginning of time. He was the embodiment of the sexual urge; it was he who caused Ouranos (the Sky) and Gaia (Earth) to generate the beings who first peopled the world. In a later tradition, however, Eros, the personification of physical love, was the son of Aphrodite, fathered by Ares; he was a beautiful, athletic young man. In the Hellenic world, he was a playful, somewhat irresponsible boy with bow and arrows. To the Romans, he was the child-god Cupid, son of Venus, the goddess whom the Romans identified with Aphrodite. While remaining an object of cult worship in the traditional religion, he was also absorbed into some of the mystery religions, as well as Christianity, that flourished in the late Hellenic and Roman worlds, as a symbol of life after death. Eventually he evolved into the cherub familiar to us from the Christian imagery of so much European medieval and Renaissance art. (And thus to his present status as a cartoon on a Valentine card.)

The Roman scholar and writer Lucius Apuleius (fl. c. 155 CE) was the author of a book called *Metamorphoses,* or *The Golden Ass,* the only novel that survives whole from the ancient world. It is a picaresque story with many bizarre adventures and entertaining digressions. One such is the fairy-tale-like story of Cupid and Psyche. Psyche ("soul") is an invention of Apuleius, but the character of Cupid is derived ultimately from the Greek Eros.

It seems that Psyche, a princess, was so beautiful that many mortals were worshiping her in Venus's place. Venus sent her son Cupid, whom Apuleius represents as a handsome young man, to cause Psyche to fall in love with a creature of monstrous ugliness, but when he saw her, Cupid fell in love with her himself. He visited her at night and became her lover, and with the help of the wind carried her off to a fairy-tale palace. He did not reveal his identity, forbidding her to look upon him in the light. One night, however, prompted by her jealous sisters, she lit a lamp as he slept, and accidentally woke him with a drop of hot oil. For her disobedience Cupid abandoned her. Heartsick, she searched for him everywhere, carrying out fantastic tasks imposed on her by Venus; but she died before finding her lover, who by that time was pleading for her with Jupiter, the supreme Roman god. Jupiter took pity, raised her to heaven and allowed her to marry Cupid.

PSYCHE

Psyche gazing on the face of Cupid for the first time.

A NOTE ON NAMES

Throughout this book, names of gods and other mythical characters, as well as places, persons, and other terms, are given in transliterated Greek form. In some cases this form is different from the more familiar Latin or Anglicized Greek form. Below is a list of names giving both forms.

TRANSLITERATED	LATIN/ANGLICIZED	TRANSLITERATED	LATIN/ANGLICIZED
Aiolia	Aeolia	Klio	Clio
Aiolos	Aeolus	Kronos	Cronos
Aischylos	Aeschylus	Kuretes	Curetes
Argos (the many-eyed)	Argus	Kyklops, Kyklopes	Cyclops, Cyclopes (plural)
Astraios	Astraeus	Leukotheia	Leucothea
Dionysos	Dionysus	Odysseos	Odysseus (Ulysses)
Epimetheos	Epimetheus	Okeanos	Oceanus, Ocean
Erebos	Erebus	Olympos	Olympus
Erechthonios	Erechthonius	Otos	Otus
Helikon	Helicon	Ourania	Urania
Hephaistos	Hephaestus	Ouranos	Uranus
Herakles	Heracles, Hercules	Parnassos	Parnassus
Hesperos	Hesperus	Phaiaka, Phaiakan	Phaiacia, Phaiacian
Iapetos	Iapetus	Plouton	Pluto
Ithaka	Ithaca	Polyphemos	Polyphemus
Kalliope	Calliope	Prometheos	Prometheus
Kallisto	Callisto	Rheia	Rhea
Kalypso	Calypso	Tartaros	Tartarus
kerykeion	caduceus		